VIRTUE STORIES

# What a Team!

Lalita Iyer

Om KIDZ

An imprint of Om Books International

A helter-skelter, watch-where-you-put-your-foot, danger-in-every-corner mess!

There was a messed up jigsaw puzzle on the floor next to a mountain of Lego. A train that had fallen off the tracks lay sprawled on the carpet. A bottle of bubble maker liquid lay half-open on the floor!

Scooby the dog was busy pulling out the insides of a teddy bear. There were beads scattered from an abandoned necklace project like the remains of an ancient archeological site. Unmade beds, towels on the floor, wherever one looked, there was chaos!

Mama entered, looked around and lost it. 'Kids, I'm telling you for the last time,' accidently stepping on a Lego piece.

'Ouch!' She screamed. 'I have had enough of this mess!'

Just then, a magna tiles house that Anya had built for her dolls, collapsed. The house was taller than she, so, naturally, it had to.'Why don't you put the toys you don't need in your toy closet?' Mama said, trying to open the cupboard.

'DON'T!' Pat and Anya screamed. It was too late.

Mama was now buried under a pile of stuffed dolls, board games, more Lego, a doll house, several balls, toy cars and hula hoops.

'Enough is enough!' She screamed.
Pin drop silence.

'I am tired of always picking up after you kids and straightening your room. If you are not going to have it spick and span in two days, I am donating all your toys and things to the thrift store. And that is that!'

She walked off in a huff. Pat, Anya and Scooby looked at each other. When Mama said, 'That is that!' it was always serious.

The room was seriously, a mess. That night at dinner, Mama was very quiet as she passed the food around. Papa was quiet too. The kids knew it was serious!

The next morning, there was a knock.

It was Papa. 'Kids, let's do this together. We are a team. Let's divide and conquer.'

Pat and Anya were excited; Scooby was, too. 'Where do we start, Papa?' Pat said, trying to figure out the beginning of the mess.

'Boxes,' said Papa. 'First, we need boxes.'

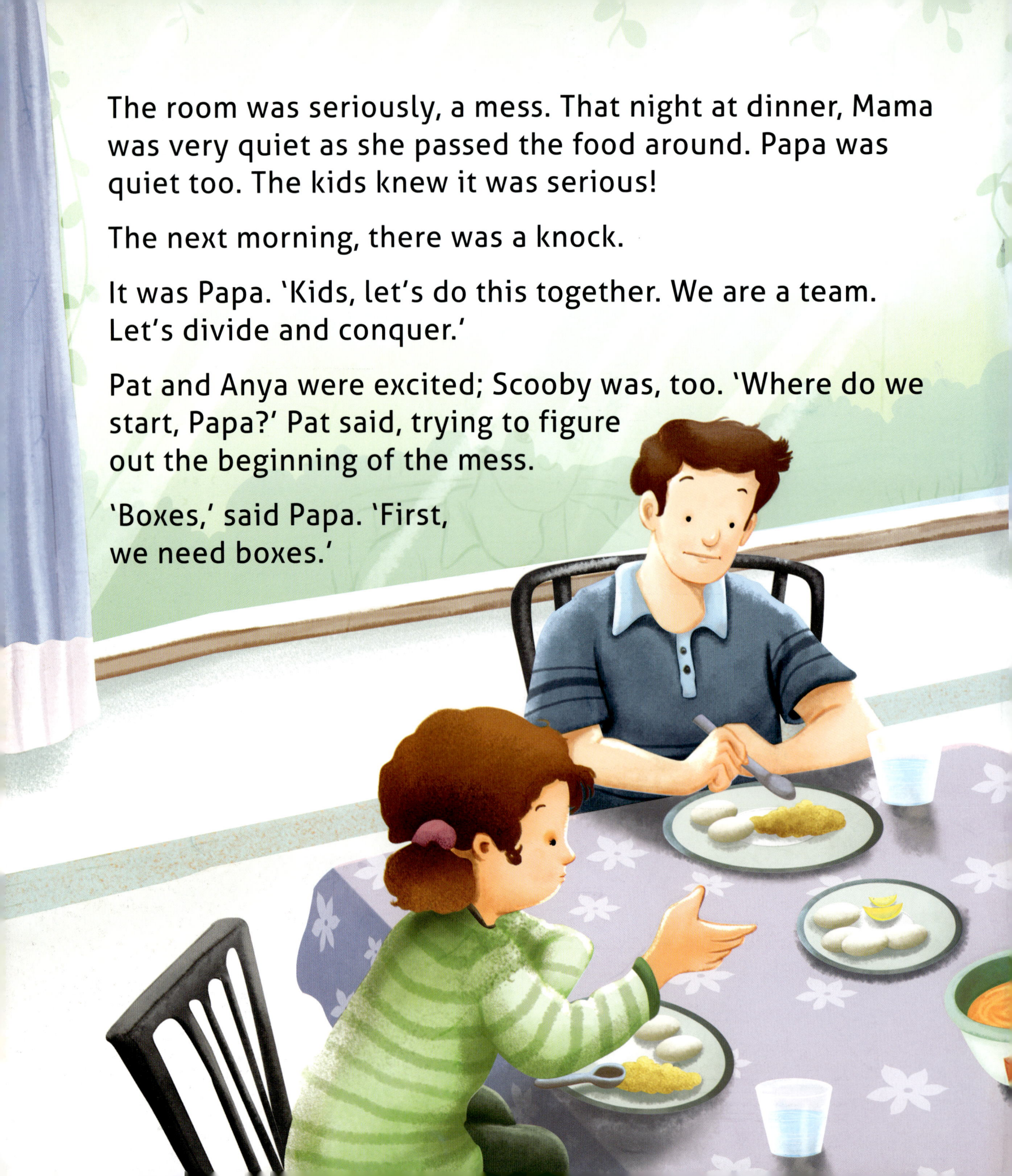

For the next two hours, Pat and Anya went about the house, collecting as many boxes as they could. They picked boxes from the basement, from the garage, and even from the study.

They now had quite a few. 'Now we need to label them and sort things into them.'

So they began labelling.

Anya had good handwriting, so she took over. Pat began the sorting.

Games. Rocks. Clay. Shells. Feathers. Pencils. Crayons. Glue. String. Model kits. Lego. Magna tiles. Puzzles. Blocks. Dolls. Doll clothes. Cards. Balls.

Gosh, they had a lot of stuff!

When they were all in boxes, it didn't look like a lot.

Even Scooby helped! He was incharge of the ball box.

And there was still some stuff that didn't belong anywhere.

'Wait!' Papa said. 'Are you willing to give this away?'

'YES!' They said.

So Papa got another box and wrote 'TO GIVE AWAY' on it.

'Next, we need to sweep this mess,' he said.

Anya, who always imagined she would fly away on a magic broom, grabbed one. 'I'll do this.'

Pat made the beds.

Just then, Mama walked in. 'What have you guys been upto? Haven't seen you all day.'

She looked at the room and couldn't believe her eyes!

'This is great work! How did you manage all this in just a day?'

Pat pointed to Anya and
Anya pointed to Scooby
and Scooby ran up to Papa
and started wagging his
tail real hard!

'It was all team work!' Papa said. 'Each one of us did something.' 'And a lot felt like a little,' said Pat and Anya.

'What a team!' said Mama, joyfully. 'The best ever!' She said, giving everyone a group hug.